The setting from the Manhattan Theatre Club production of "The Wash." Set design by James Youmans

THE WASH

PHILIP KAN GOTANDA

★

★

DRAMATISTS
PLAY SERVICE
INC.

THE WASH was originally written for the Japanese American Citizens League
sponsored by Henry and Chiyo Kuwahata Arts Grant.

THE WASH was produced as a workshop in the 1985 New Theatre for Now Festival
at the Mark Taper Forum. Gordon Davidson, Artistic Director/Producer.

THE WASH was originally produced at the Eureka Theatre Company of
San Francisco in 1987.

THE WASH was originally produced in New York by Manhattan Theatre Club, City Center
Stage II, in association with the Mark Taper Forum, on October 23, 1990.

SOUND EFFECTS
The following is a list of sound effects referenced in this play:
Telephone ring
Baby cry
Telephone answering machine beep
Coffee grinder

SPECIAL NOTE ON SONGS AND RECORDINGS
For performance of the songs, arrangements and recordings mentioned in this Play that are protected by copyright, the permission of the copyright owners must be obtained; or other songs, arrangements and recordings in the public domain substituted.

THE WASH was produced at the Manhattan Theatre Club (Lynne Meadow, Artistic Director; Barry Grove, Managing Director) in New York City on October 23, 1990. It was directed by Sharon Ott; the set design was by James Youmans; the costume design was by Lydia Tanji; the lighting design was by Dan Kotlowitz; the original music and sound was by Stephen LeGrand and the production stage manager was Renee Lutz. The cast was as follows:

NOBU MATSUMOTO	Sab Shimono
MASI MATSUMOTO	Nobu McCarthy
MARSHA MATSUMOTO	Diane Takei
JUDY ADAMS	Jodi Long
KIYOKO HASEGAWA	Shizuko Hoshi
BLACKIE	Marshall Factora
SADAO NAKASATO	George Takei
CHIYO FROELICH	Carol A. Honda

THE WASH was produced at the Mark Taper Forum (Gordon Davidson, Artistic Director; Stephen J. Albert, Managing Director) in Los Angeles, California, on January 6, 1991. It was directed by Sharon Ott; the set design was by James Youmans; the costume design was by Lydia Tanji; the lighting design was by Paulie Jenkins; the original music and sound was by Stephen LeGrand and Eric Drew Feldman and the production stage manager was Cari Norton. The cast was as follows:

NOBU MATSUMOTO	Sab Shimono
MASI MATSUMOTO	Nobu McCarthy
MARSHA MATSUMOTO	Diane Takei
JUDY ADAMS	Jodi Long
KIYOKO HASEGAWA	Shizuko Hoshi
BLACKIE SAKATA	James Saito
SADAO NAKASATO	George Takei
CHIYO FROELICH	Carol A. Honda

THE WASH was originally written for the Japanese American Citizens League sponsored Henry & Chiyo Kuwahara Arts Council and was originally produced at the Eureka Theatre Company of San Francisco. It was produced as a workshop at the Mark Taper Forum as part of the 1985 New Theatre for Now Festival.

CHARACTERS

NOBU MATSUMOTO

"Nisei" (2nd generation Japanese American). 68 years old. Retired produce man. Separated from wife, Masi. Lives alone in the family house.

MASI MATSUMOTO

"Nisei." 67 years old. Left Nobu. Does housework for a living. Lives in a small apartment by herself.

KIYOKO HASEGAWA

55-ish. Originally from Japan. Previously married to an American soldier. Widow. Seeing Nobu. Owns and runs a small Japanese restaurant.

SADAO NAKASATO

"Nisei." 65 years old. Widower. Seeing Masi. Retired pharmacist.

MARSHA MATSUMOTO

"Sansei" (3rd generation Japanese American). 33 years old. Single. Older daughter of Nobu and Masi. Works as a dental hygienist in a nearby big city.

JUDY ADAMS

"Sansei." 29 years old. Married to James with a baby. Younger daughter of Nobu and Masi. 5th grade teacher. Presently not working.

CHIYO FROELICH

Originally from Japan, but has lived most of her adult life in the U.S. Late 40's. Divorced. Friend of Kiyoko. Owns and runs small beauty salon next door to Kiyoko's restaurant.

CURLEY SAKATA

Hawaiian "Nisei." 55-ish. Speaks with a thick pidgin that comes and goes at his convenience. Works as the cook at Kiyoko's restaurant.

SETTING

Center is Nobu's place, the "old family home." Stage Right is Kiyoko's restaurant. Stage Left is Masi's small apartment. The clothesline is in the upstage area. The down area is used to play several scenes that take place elsewhere.

The set should be realistic but elemental, allowing for an underlying abstract feeling. Nobu's place is the most complete, with Masi's and Kiyoko's places more minimal.

The play takes place in the present over a period of 6 months – July to January. Clothing that reflects the seasonal changes might assist in showing the passage of time.

THE WASH

ACT ONE

Scene 1

Nobu's place, the old family home. Along the U. area is the kitchen. L. is a door that leads to the outside, the proverbial side door entrance into the kitchen that everyone uses. R. of the kitchen along the U. side is a door leading to the hall-way and bedrooms, a sink, refrigerator, stove. There is a kitchen table with a pile of dirty clothes on it. On the stove, a pot of water is boiling.

In the washrack there is a teapot, some dishes, chopsticks, etc. D.R. a TV is on quietly. A long couch is angled facing the TV. A long coffee table in front of couch. On it sits the yet undeveloped skeleton of a large kite Nobu is building. Throughout the course of the play, the kite becomes more and more pronounced in its construction.

The pile of dirty clothes is lit in a shaft of light. Lights come up to half on Nobu's place. Nobu asleep, lengthwise on the couch, facing the TV. Newspaper is sprawled over his chest. Mouth open, snoring loudly. TV lights come up. Nobu can be seen in the flickering light of the television screen. Lights come full up. Nobu awakens with a start, newspaper falling to the floor. Pulls himself upright and just sits and stares into space for a moment, trying to awaken.

Then picks up the newspaper, tosses it in a heap on the couch. Checks to examine the progress he's making on the kite. Carefully sets the kite back on table and shuffles over to the stove to shut the boiling water off. He gets a plate and a pair of chopsticks from the washrack, puts the two hotdogs that were boiling onto the plate. Then he gets some tea out and puts it into the teapot which he has taken from the rack. About to throw out the hotdog water to boil some new water, then stops. Thinking. Proceeds to just pour the hotdog water into the teapot and use it to make tea.

Nobu reaches into the refrigerator and pulls out a bowl of cold rice, covered over in cellophane, and a small bottle of French's Mustard. He uncovers the rice, scoops some of it into a rice bowl using his chopsticks, pours hot tea over it. It starts to spill, quickly bends down and slurps up the excess. He opens the mustard and using his chopsticks again, shovels a healthy portion of mustard onto his hotdogs. Licks the mustard off his chopsticks. Then he carefully makes his way back to the couch with the plate of hotdogs and a bowl of rice. Sets the food down on the coffee table and begins to eat while working on the kite and watching television.

While he is eating, Masi enters through the side door with two large brown paper bags. She's struggling to open and close the door with both hands so full. Nobu turns around and notices her but gives no greeting and makes no effort to help her. Instead, goes back to eating, working on the kite and watching TV. She is not upset by his actions. She appears to have no expectation of assistance from him. Business as usual. Masi sets both bags on the kitchen table and catches her breath. She proceeds to put vegetables from one of the bags into the refrigerator. Tomatoes and Japanese eggplant.

MASI. *(Putting vegetables into refrigerator.)* If you have any more dirty clothes I can take them now. Nobu? Is this everything?
NOBU. *(Not turning, eating.)* Want some hotdog?
MASI. No, I ate before. Got these from Mr. Rossi. The tomatoes are soft so eat them right away. *(Folds bag and puts it into*

a drawer. She knows this place well. Walks over and checks his shirt collar from behind.) No more clothes?

NOBU. *(Brushing her hand away.)* No already. *(Masi goes over to the other bag and begins unpacking the freshly washed clothes in neat piles on the kitchen table.)*

MASI. *(Unpacking.)* I just finished cleaning Dr. Harrison's place. You should see the bathrooms. If you see the family walk down the street, they look so clean and neat. But the toilets, "kitanai" [dirty]. *(Finished unpacking, Masi takes a cup out of the rack and pours herself a cup of tea. She walks over to the couch and sits down next to Nobu and watches TV. She takes a sip of tea and makes a face. Nobu notices.)*

NOBU. Hotdog water. *(Masi decides not to drink. She looks at the unfinished kite frame.)*

MASI. You gonna fly this one? *(Picking up the kite.)* Nobu, why don't you at least try a different design this ...

NOBU. My old man did it this way. *(Mutters.)* Jesus Christ ...

MASI. *(Gathering clothes.)* Have you talked to the kids? *(No response.)* Marsha said she stopped by. *(Beat.)* You know if you don't see Judy's baby soon he's going to be all grown up. Nobu?

NOBU. No. *(Masi gives up trying to talk to him at all.)*

MASI. No more dirty clothes, Nobu? *(Nobu shakes his head without turning away from the TV.)* Alright, then I'm going. *(Masi leaves with the bag of old clothes. Nobu continues to watch TV for a few moments. Then, turns and stares at the door. Dim to half, with the TV light illuminating Nobu. Marsha lit in pool of light looking towards Nobu.)*

MARSHA. Dad? *(Nobu turns to look at Marsha momentarily, then back to the television. Judy is lit in a pool of light, holding Timothy.)*

JUDY. Mom? *(Masi moving away. Masi turns to look at Judy momentarily, then exits. Marsha and Judy dim to darkness. Nobu and Masi dim to darkness. We hear Japanese restaurant muzak.)*

Scene 2

Kiyoko's restaurant. Afternoon, next day. Lights come up. Kiyoko struggling to move Chiyo's "Karaoke"* equipment out of the way.

KIYOKO. *(Calling.)* Curley! Curley can you help me with this! *(Curley Sakata enters, wiping face with towel and holding beer. Speaks with an Hawaiian pidgin. He can lose it if he wants to.)*

CURLEY. Easy, easy, no go break da speaker. Bumbye Curley's sweet sounds no can come out. *(Helping her move the equipment.)*

KIYOKO. *(Struggling.)* Why can't Chiyo keep this at her place?

CURLEY. Hey, cannot sing karaoke at a beauty shop. Has to be night club place like dis.

KIYOKO. This is a restaurant ... *(As they finish moving the equipment, Kiyoko notices Curley's beer. Stares at him.)*

CURLEY. *(Feigning innocence.)* What's-a-matta?

KIYOKO. Curley.

CURLEY. It makes my cooking mo' betta. *(Kiyoko stares, no response.)* It makes me mo' betta. *(Kiyoko continues to stare.)* I'm thirsty, I wanted a beer.

KIYOKO. *(Taking his beer.)* No more drinking on the job, I told you.

CURLEY. But it makes my cooking mo' betta. If I feel betta, my cooking mo' betta. No bull lie "yo."

KIYOKO. *(Scooting Curley back to the kitchen.)* Your face turns red like a tomato and everything tastes like "shoyu" [soy sauce].

CURLEY. *(Exiting into the back, scratching his behind.)* This place no fun no mo'.

KIYOKO. And don't scratch your "oshiri," you're the cook,

---

* Japanese singing accompaniment machine.

remember? *(As Kiyoko goes back to wiping, Nobu enters and walks up to Kiyoko. Noticing.)* "Irasshaii" [welcome].

NOBU. *(Holds out his hand to her.)* Excuse me. Here. *(Kiyoko doesn't know what's going on. Taking Kiyoko's hand and giving her money.)* Here, here, you gave me too much. You gave me too much change. When I paid my bill. I was emptying out my pockets at my house when I noticed.

KIYOKO. *(Looking at the money.)* Twenty-five cents?

NOBU. *(Nodding.)* Uh-huh. It cost six seventy-five, I gave you seven bucks and you gave me back fifty cents. So ... *(Nobu nods towards the money. He's not sure what to do next. Awkward beat. Then turns to leave.)*

KIYOKO. Wait, wait. *(Nobu stops. Beat. For a moment Kiyoko doesn't know what to say.)* You walked all the way back here to give me 25 cents?

NOBU. You gave me too much. So I ... *(Kiyoko doesn't know what to say.)* Alright then. *(Nobu turns to leave again.)*

KIYOKO. No, wait, wait. Sit, sit, please sit. I'll get you some tea. *(Kiyoko guides him to a seat and goes to get his tea. Curley has been watching the action. Sipping on a new beer.)*

CURLEY. Eh, Mr. Abe Lincoln? You come in a lot, huh. For lunch.

NOBU. Almost every day.

CURLEY. *(Approaching.)* And dat's your seat, huh? All da time you gotta sit in dat same seat. Last week Mr. Koyama was sitting dere — I saw you come in — you left and came back later when dat seat was open. What's a-matta, your butt got a magnet for dat seat?

KIYOKO. *(Bringing tea, shooing Curley away.)* Curley. Go, go ...

CURLEY. *(Moving away, to Nobu.)* And you always order da same thing.

NOBU. The combo plate.

KIYOKO. And you like the eggplant pickle.

NOBU. Un-huh.

KIYOKO. Kagoshima style.

NOBU. "Kagoshima ka?" My family's from there.

KIYOKO. "Ara, Kagoshima? Honto, yo?" [From Kagoshima? Really?] "Doko kara," where?

11

NOBU. The, uh, southern part.

KIYOKO. Ahhh. "Watashi no," north part, Yokokawa. *(Awkward beat. Motioning to his tea.)* "Dozo" [please]. *(Nobu sips the tea.)* What is your name?

NOBU. *(Getting up.)* Nobu. Nobu Matsumoto.

KIYOKO. Ah, Matsumoto-san. Kiyoko. Kiyoko Hasegawa. "Dozo yoroshiku." [How do you do.] *(As Nobu starts to awkwardly bow, Kiyoko extends her hand to shake. He's caught off guard and both are slightly embarrassed. Nobu recovers and reaches out to shake Kiyoko's hand. Curley watches, amused. Dim to darkness.)*

Scene 3

Masi's place. 3 weeks later. Small apartment with bedroom down stage from main room. Sadao is lit seated on sofa in a pool of light. Masi is in half light at counter fixing coffee.

SADAO. We were all sitting around in somebody's living room, when someone said, "How come you still wear your wedding ring?" They weren't being mean. That's why we were there. To ask those kinds of things. I didn't know what to say. Speechless. Then someone else said, "Sadao, you always complain about not meeting people not being able to start a new life — how come you still wear your ring?" I began to cry. Like a little boy. I remember thinking, "How strange. I am crying in front of all these people that I don't know. And yet I feel no shame. The room was so still. All you could hear was my crying. Then I heard a tapping sound. I looked up and noticed a woman sitting across from me, slapping the sandals she was wearing against the bottom of her feet. Tap, tap, tap. ... I said I didn't know why. It just never crossed my mind to take it off. "Why should I take the ring off?" Then one of the widows, the one who formed the group said, "Because you're not married anymore." *(Lights come up on the rest of the apartment area. Masi is at the small kitchen counter fixing 2 cups of Sanka coffee. She wasn't quite prepared for him sharing such personal*

*details of his life and is a bit unsure how to respond. Sadao in turn
fears he may have gotten a bit carried away.)*

MASI. *(Bringing coffee over.)* Cream? It's non-dairy creamer.
(Sadao shakes head.) If you want tea?

SADAO. No, this is fine. I ran on a bit, didn't I?

MASI. No, no, it's alright. *(Pause.)* It's just Sanka.

SADAO. Good. Otherwise the caffeine keeps me up all night.
Have you tried decaffeinated coffee? *(Masi motions to the Sanka,
unsure of what he means.)* No, the bean. They actually make a
decaffeinated bean.

MASI. No, we never did anything like that. Just instant.
Yuban makes a good instant coffee. That's what I usually
drink. But I don't have any since I moved over here.

SADAO. No, I've never tried it.

MASI. I'll have to get some next time I go shopping.

SADAO. They have this process they use. On the bean. I
mean they don't grow a decaffeinated bean. I don't know
what's worse. The caffeine in it or the chemicals they use to
get the caffeine out. *(Laughing at his own joke. Gathering momen-
tum.)* I have a little grinder. Braun? You know a Braun? *(Masi
doesn't know what it is. Awkward pause.)*

MASI. We never did anything like that. We just drink instant.

SADAO. I like Sanka. I have to drink it all the time. Doctor's
orders. *(Imitating.)* "If you drink coffee, Sadao, drink Sanka!"
*(Laughs valiantly at his attempt at humor. Masi stares at her cup.
Sadao notices and offers a feeble explanation.)* Blood pressure ...
(They both drink in silence. Suddenly, Sadao remembers something.)
Oh, I forgot. *(Sadao reaches down and picks up a fishing pole and
reel wrapped up like presents.)*

MASI. *(Surprised.)* Sadao, what's this? *(Sadao holds out pole.)* I
can't. *(Nobu lit in a half-light at his place watching TV. His face
illuminated by the flickering screen's glow.)*

SADAO. No, no, it's for *you.*

MASI. But Sadao ...

SADAO. No, no, it's for *you.*

MASI. *(One hand on it.)* Sadao, you shouldn't have.

SADAO. Go 'head. Open it up.

MASI. *(Takes it and begins unwrapping it.)* No, I can't accept

13

this. I don't have anything for you. (*Masi unwraps pole, which is broken down into pieces. Sadao sets reel on table and takes pole from Masi and proceeds to put it together.*)

SADAO. Here, let me show you. (*Puts it together.*) There. (*Hands it back. Remembers reel, hands it to her. Masi takes reel. She now has a reel and pole in both hands. Sadao realizes she can't unwrap it with both hands full and takes pole away so she can unwrap the reel. She unwraps it. Sadao promptly takes it away from her hand and puts the pole and reel together.*) See, it goes like this. And then you're all set to catch fish. (*Hands it back to Masi.*) I told you I was going to take you. Now you can't refuse.

MASI. Yeah, but ...

SADAO. Thought I was kidding, huh?

MASI. But this is so expensive. I know how much these things cost, 'cause of Nobu. I don't know anything about fishing. He's the fisherman. I just pack the lunch and off he goes.

SADAO. Well, this time you're going and it's lots of fun. Economical, too. You get to eat what you catch.

MASI. But you have to do all that walking.

SADAO. No, who said that? We sit on the bank and fish from there. We'll pack a good lunch — I'll make it — you bring the cards so we can play Blackjack. We have to practice.

MASI. I don't play.

SADAO. That's why we have to practice so we can go to Tahoe. If there's a good game on we'll have to watch it. I'll bring my portable TV. I love the Giants.

MASI. What about fishing?

SADAO. Only if we have time. See, this is how you cast out. (*Demonstrating.*) You hook your index finger around the line here. Turn the bail and ... (*Casts. Nobu still lit in half-light, gets up to phone Masi. Phone rings. Masi goes over and answers it. It's Nobu. Slowly lights dim on Sadao and rest of the apartment. Masi and Nobu are lit.*)

MASI. Hello.

NOBU. (*Lit in small pool of light.*) You coming to pick up the clothes?

MASI. Nobu? I was just there. You mean next week? Don't

14

worry, I'll be there. I do it every week, don't I? Nobu?

NOBU. I'm not worried. You alright?

MASI. Yes, I'm alright. Did you want something? *(No response.)* I got more vegetables. Do you need some more?

NOBU. No. *(Pause.)* Can you bring more eggplant?

MASI. I don't have anymore.

NOBU. Alright then.

MASI. I'll ask Mr. Rossi. He can always get lots more. *(Pause.)* Nobu, I have to go now.

NOBU. I went fishing so I got a lot of dirty clothes.

MASI. Alright. Don't worry, I'll be by.

NOBU. I'm not worried.

MASI. Bye.

NOBU. Bye. *(Dim to darkness.)*

Scene 4

Poker game. Curley setting up Karaoke machine. Chiyo and Kiyoko at table. Chiyo dealing out cards. Wears a poker visor. Playing 5 card stud. One card down and one up.

CHIYO. Kiyoko, I never said I didn't like him.

CURLEY. *(Fiddling with the machine.)* Test, test.

KIYOKO. Curley, you in this game or not?

CURLEY. *(Singing into microphone.)* "Tiny bubbles ..."

CHIYO. I just don't think he's right for you, that's all. He's too old.

KIYOKO. Curley, we're waiting.

CURLEY. Okay, okay.

CHIYO. Dealer's high, I bet a nickel.

KIYOKO. I see you. *(Curley moves to table, guzzling a beer and carrying a 6 pack in his other hand. They both notice Curley chugging down the rest of his beer. Making loud gurgling sounds. Curley notices them staring.)*

CURLEY. You gotta drink beer when you're playing poker or you aren't playing poker. You're just playing cards. I don't like cards. Hate cards. *(Holds up another beer.)* I "love" poker.

15

KIYOKO. *(To Curley.)* Ante, ante ...

CHIYO. Go dancing with Eddie and me, yeah come, come ...

KIYOKO. Chiyo, how can I do that? Who's gunna run this place, huh?

CHIYO. Come on, Kiyoko, you work too hard.

KIYOKO. The refrigeration unit's breaking down, Mr. Sato says we can't fix it anymore —

CHIYO. Kiyoko, I met one of Eddie's friends, Ray Jensen, he's good looking yo'. Tall, lottsa fun to be with —

KIYOKO. Chiyo, Chiyo, I'm too busy. I'm not looking for that kind of thing anymore.

CHIYO. What do you mean, 'That kind of thing?'

KIYOKO. That kind of thing, thinking about men and getting all ...

CURLEY. I like it when da wahinis talk dirt. *(Kiyoko and Chiyo shoot Curley a dirty look.)* Geez, don't lose your coconut.

KIYOKO. I like Nobu, he's a nice man, Chiyo. He comes in here, we sit down and eat together and then he goes home. I like that.

CHIYO. *(To Kiyoko.)* Okay, Okay. Two 6's, a pair of saxophones. *(To Curley.)* A 3 of diamonds gives you ... nothing. *(To self.)* 8 of puppy toes to the dealer, working on a possible club flush. *(To Kiyoko.)* Pair of saxes high. He's married Kiyoko.

KIYOKO. Ten cents. They're separated.

CHIYO. But did he tell you. Huh? I call.

KIYOKO. Curley, you in or not?

CURLEY. Don't rush me, don't rush me.

CHIYO. No, you had to hear it from me. 80 year old Mrs. Nakamura with the blue hair comes to my beauty shop, "I want my perm and a blue rinse," yak-yaking away. I decide to do some snooping for my good friend. "Nakamura-san? Oh, Nakamura-san? You know this Nobu guy?"

CURLEY. Old magnet butt?

CHIYO. I know his kind, Kiyoko. Old Japanese-type guys. She left him, he can't get over that. He's still thinking about her. He only wants you for one thing — your tempura. Yeah. He's over here everyday "desho" [isn't he]. You feeding him. He's eating up all your profits.

KIYOKO. Chiyo.

CHIYO. *(To Kiyoko.)* 9 of spades. No help there. *(To Curley.)* A trois. Oh, a pair of 3's. *(To self.)* And for the dealer ... another club. Flush looking very possible. *(To Kiyoko.)* Pair of saxes still high.

KIYOKO. Check.

CHIYO. Check. He checks too.

CURLEY. I'm thinking, I'm thinking ...

CHIYO. I try looking out for you and what do you do? You get mad at me.

KIYOKO. Nobu is an honest man. That's all I know. One time I gave him too much change, he walked all the way ...

CURLEY. *(Overlapping, mimicking Kiyoko.)* — he walked all the way back to return it. Twenty-five cents.

CHIYO. *(Overlapping Curley, mimicking Kiyoko, too.)* — to return it. Twenty-five cents. *(Curley and Chiyo laugh.)* Good investment. He gets a $4.50 combo plate free now. Last card, down and dirty. *(Chiyo starts dealing as she and Curley calm down.)*

KIYOKO. Look, he's just a friend. That's all he is. I don't see why you're all making such a fuss.

CHIYO. *(Showing her card.)* Another puppy toes – flush, flush, flush.

KIYOKO. 50 cents.

CURLEY. *(Surprised.)* 50 cents.

CHIYO. *(Confidentially.)* I see you and I bump you one dollar.

CURLEY. *(In disbelief.)* One dollar ... *(Kiyoko eyes Chiyo's cards and tries to decide whether to stay in or not.)*

KIYOKO. I call you.

CHIYO. You got the 3-of-a-kind?

KIYOKO. Pair of sixes, that's all. You got the flush?

CHIYO. Pair of eights! Hah! *(Chiyo's about to grab the pot when Curley puts down his cards.)*

CURLEY. Excusez-moi's, but I got 3 trois's.

CHIYO. Curley ...

KIYOKO. Oh, Curley ...

CURLEY. *(Holding up beer.)* Hate cards. "Love" poker. *(Dim to darkness.)*

Scene 5

Nobu's place. Marsha's dinner party scene. Marsha busy at stove. Nobu seated in his chair.

NOBU. What do you mean, 'be nice to Mama'?

MARSHA. All I'm saying is just try to be nice to her when she gets here. Say something nice about the way she looks or about the way she dresses —

NOBU. I'm always nice to Mama. I'm always good to her. *(Marsha moving over to Nobu and adjusting his clothes.)*

MARSHA. Dad, Dad, I just want us to have a good time tonight, OK? All of us, together. And besides, I made you your favorite. *(Marsha moving back to stove.)*

NOBU. Yeah, but how come Mama has to live over there, huh? She should be at home here. How come Mama has to live way in the hell over there? *(Masi enters carrying a small paper bag.)*

MARSHA. Hi Mom. *(Taking bag.)* Here let me take that.

MASI. *(To Nobu.)* Just some left-over fruit that was in the ice-box. Starting to rot so eat it right away. And this is for you. *(Masi hands package to Marsha. Masi and Nobu acknowledge each other awkwardly.)*

MARSHA. Thanks, Mom. *(Takes package.)* Judy and the baby couldn't make it.

MASI. She called me.

NOBU. Eh? *(Nobu's expression reveals he didn't know they were coming.)*

MARSHA. *(Offering explanation to Nobu.)* Jimmy wasn't going to come. *(Pause.)* Sit down, sit down. Dinner's almost ready in a minute. Roast beef. Dad, coffee? Tea, for you Mom? *(Marsha goes to kitchen. Silence.)*

NOBU. She wanted to eat at her place. I told her to cook dinner here. *(Pause.)*

MASI. Her place is cozy, "neh."

NOBU. Marsha's? Looks like the rooms back in Camp.

MASI. At least she's clean. Not like the younger one. *(Pause.)*

NOBU. How you been?

MASI. Alright.

NOBU. 'Isogashii no?" [Busy?]

MASI. No. The usual.

NOBU. I called the other night, no one answered. *(Masi doesn't offer an explanation.)* How you been? *(Marsha interrupts, carrying an ashtray.)*

MARSHA. Dad, look what Mom gave me. She's taking a ceramics class. Judy got her to go. *(Hands him the ashtray.)* She made it. *(Nobu stares at it.)*

MASI. It's an ashtray.

NOBU. You don't smoke.

MASI. I'll get Daddy's coffee. *(Masi exits with cup.)*

MARSHA. Dad, just say you like it. That's all you have to say. Just say it's nice.

NOBU. Yeah, but you don't smoke. Why give an ashtray if you don't smoke? *(Masi returns with a cup of coffee for Nobu and tea for herself. Marsha gives Nobu an encouraging nudge and exits into kitchen. Holding ashtray.)* It's a nice ashtray. Is this where you go all the time? I call in the evening. I guess that's where you must be. *(Pause.)* Remember those dances they used to have in the Camps? You were a good dancer. You were. Best in the Camps.

MASI. You couldn't dance at all. You were awful.

NOBU. Remember that fellow Chester Yoshikawa? That friend of yours?

MASI. He could dance so good.

NOBU. Remember that dance you were supposed to meet me out front of the canteen? We were all going to meet there and then go to the dance together. Shig, Chester, and a couple of others. Everybody else, they went on ahead. I waited and waited ...

MASI. Nobu, that was 40 years ago.

NOBU. Yeah, I know but remember you were supposed to meet ...

MASI. *(Interrupts.)* That's over 40 years ago. How can I remember something like that?

NOBU. You didn't show up. Chester didn't show up either. *(Masi puts cream and sugar into Nobu's coffee.)*

19

MASI. Nobu, didn't we talk about this? I'm sure we did. Probably something came up and I had to help Mama and Papa.

NOBU. Where were you, huh?

MASI. How am I supposed to remember that far back? Chester died in Italy with the rest of the 442 boys.

NOBU. Where the hell were you?

MASI. How in the hell am I supposed to remember that far back! *(Nobu notices his coffee.)*

NOBU. *You* put the cream and sugar in. That's not mine. *(Pushes coffee away. Masi realizes what she's done.)*

MASI. That's right. You like to put the cream and sugar in yourself.

NOBU. I like to put it in myself.

MASI. *(Pushing cup towards him.)* It's the way you like it, the same thing.

NOBU. *(Pushes it back. Marsha pokes her head in and watches.)* No, it's not the same thing.

MASI. Alright, alright, I'll drink it myself. Here, you can drink mine. *(Masi shoves her tea to Nobu and grabs the coffee cup.)*

NOBU. What are you doing?

MASI. I don't mind. *(Masi starts to raise cup, but Nobu reaches for it.)*

NOBU. It's no good for you Mama. Your blood pressure. Remember what Doc Tanaka ...

MASI. *(Interrupts. Clinging to cup.)* Who gives a damn. You make such a fuss about it. "Monku, monku, monku" [kvetch, kvetch, kvetch]. — I'll drink it.

NOBU. *(Struggling with Masi.)* It's no good for you Mama. *(Coffee spills on the table. To Masi.)* Clean it up.

MASI. I'm not going to clean it up.

MARSHA. *(Entering.)* I'll clean it up. *(While Marsha starts to wipe the table, Masi grabs Nobu's coffee cup and exits into the kitchen.)*

MASI. *(Exiting.)* I'll get him more coffee.

MARSHA. Dad.

NOBU. That's the way she is. *(Masi returns with Nobu's coffee and sets it down in front of him. Then, she turns and quickly exits.)*

MARSHA. *(Chasing after Masi.)* Mom. *(Nobu is left alone with his cup of coffee. Marsha reenters and watches him as he slowly puts in the cream and sugar himself. Raises the cup to his lips but cannot drink. Sets it back down and stares at it. Marsha continues to watch him. Dim to darkness.)*

Scene 6

That same night. After hours at the restaurant. Chiyo and Curley with microphones singing a song like "Sukiyaki"* to the accompaniment of the Karaoke machine. Curley begins to do the hula. Kiyoko laughing and clapping along. They're all having a good time. Nobu enters. He wasn't expecting this and is not sure what to do. As Chiyo continues to sing, Curley notices him.

CURLEY. *(Calling.)* Nobu! Nobu! *(Kiyoko goes up to Nobu who is turning to leave.)*

KIYOKO. *(Catching him and trying to make him enter.)* Nobu, come in, come in — Chiyo and Curley set up the machine and we're all singing ... *(Nobu doesn't budge. Kiyoko notices that he is upset about something. Gently.)* Nobu? Sit down. Come in for a while. Sit, sit. I'll get you a beer. *(Kiyoko leads the reluctant Nobu to his seat as Chiyo and Curley continue to sing. Kiyoko clears the table and goes back up to the counter for his beer. Chiyo and Curley have just finished their song and are now teasing Nobu to also join in.)*

CURLEY. Come on, your turn Nobu.

CHIYO. Sing, sing.

CURLEY. It's Karaoke night at Hasegawa's!

CHIYO. "Ojiisan, doozo!" [Old man, please!]

CHIYO and CURLEY. *(Chanting.)* Nobu, Nobu, Nobu ... *(Kiyoko returning with his beer.)*

---

* See Special Note on copyright page.

KIYOKO. Chiyo, Curley, leave him alone, leave him alone ... *(They stop, move back to the Karaoke machine.)*
CURLEY. *(Muttering.)* What a bugga.
KIYOKO. *(To Nobu.)* Tsukemono? *(Nobu nods and Kiyoko exits. Nobu is left alone. He sits for a moment in silence. Then, he begins to quietly sing. First softly, then growing in volume.)*
 Nen nen kororiyo okororiyo
 Bōya wa yoi ko da nen ne shina
 Bōya yo mari wa doko e itta
 Ano yama koete sato e itta.
[Translation:
 Sleep, sleep, hushabye
 Little boy, good boy, go to sleep now
 Little boy, where has your ball gone?
 Way over the mountains to the distant fields.]
CURLEY. What's he singing?
CHIYO. I don't know.
KIYOKO. It's a lullaby. *(Chiyo and Curley start to laugh at Nobu singing a baby's song.)* Shh! Shh! *(Hearing them, Nobu stops. Kiyoko starts to sing to help Nobu out. Nobu joins back in. Nobu's voice is not pretty. But it is earnest and straight forward, filling the traditional song with a gutsy soulfulness. Kiyoko and Nobu finish the song together.)*
NOBU. *(Quietly.)* My Papa used to sing it to me. *(Dim to darkness.)*

Scene 7

Masi's place. 3 weeks later. Afternoon. Masi at clothesline. Judy visiting with Timothy.

JUDY. I don't see how you had two of us, Mom. I need sleep. Large doses of it. Jimmy's so lazy sometimes. I even kick him "accidentally" when Timothy starts crying. Think he gets up to feed the baby?
MASI. Daddy used to.
JUDY. Used to what?

MASI. Get up at night and feed you kids.

JUDY. Dad? You're kidding.

MASI. He used to sing to you. No wonder you kids would cry. *(They laugh.)*

JUDY. I saw your new phone answering machine.

MASI. *(Proud.)* Yeah. For messages.

JUDY. *(Kidding.)* What? You got a new boyfriend?

MASI. Judy.

JUDY. Well, why not Mom? You moved out. It's about time you started meeting new people. Once you get a divorce you're going to have to do that any ...

MASI. *(Interrupts.)* I'm not getting a divorce.

JUDY. What are you going to do? You live here, Dad's over there ... *(No response.)* You can't do that forever.

MASI. I just do his wash. That's all I do. Just his wash. *(Pause. Masi hanging clothes.)* I think you should call Dad.

JUDY. Mom, what can I say to him? I can't talk about my husband, I can't talk about my baby.

MASI. Judy, you know how Dad is.

JUDY. All he can talk about is how he can't show his face at Tak's barber shop because I married a "kurochan" [black].

MASI. He's not going to call you.

JUDY. Of course not — we'd have to talk. *(Silence. Judy goes back to the baby. Masi watches her.)*

MASI. Judy.

JUDY. What?

MASI. He needs you.

JUDY. Why can't he accept it. Why can't he just say, "it's OK, it's OK Judy"? I just need him to say that much.

MASI. He can't. Papa can't.

JUDY. Why? Why the hell not? *(Masi and Judy look at each other. Dim to darkness.)*

Scene 8

Kiyoko's Restaurant. That same evening. We hear the rhythmic pounding of fists on flesh. As lights come up, Nobu and Kiyoko are lit in a pool of light. Kiyoko is standing in back of Nobu pounding his back with fists in a punching manner. She is massaging Nobu. This is a supreme joy for him. Kiyoko likes doing it for him.

KIYOKO. *(Not stopping.)* Enough?
NOBU. *(Voice vibrating from the steady blows.)* Nooo ... *(They continue in silence, both enjoying the activity.)*
KIYOKO. Enough?
NOBU. Noo ... *(Kiyoko's arms are just too tired.)*
KIYOKO. *(Stopping.)* Ahh ...
NOBU. *(Stretching.)* "Oisho!" [Ahh!] Masi used to do it. Sometimes Marsha does it now.
KIYOKO. *(Pouring tea.)* You're lucky you have children, Nobu. Especially daughters. Harry and I wanted children. They're good, neh. *(Awkward silence. Nobu abruptly pulls out a small gift-wrapped box and holds it out to Kiyoko.)*
NOBU. Here. *(Kiyoko's too surprised to take it. From here, spoken in Japanese, except where otherwise indicated.)* "Anata no birthday present. Hayo akenasai." [Your birthday present. Hurry, open it.]
KIYOKO. *(Taking it.)* "Ara! Nobu ..." *(Opens it and holds up the earrings.)* Nobu-chan.
NOBU. Earrings. Inamasu Jewelry Store "no mae o totara me ni tsuitanda ne." [I was walking by Inamasu's store when I spotted them.]
KIYOKO. "Mah, kirei, Nobu-chan. Tsukete miru." [They're pretty Nobu. Let me try them on.] *(Kiyoko exits. Nobu lit in pool of light. Memory sequence: Masi lit in pool of light.)*
MASI. Why don't you want me anymore? *(No response.)* We don't sleep.... You know what I mean and don't give me that kind of look. Is it me? The way my body.... I've seen those magazines you keep in the back closet with your fishing and

24

hunting gear. I mean, it's alright. I'm just trying to know about us. What happened.

NOBU. Nothing. Nothing happened. What's the matter with you?

MASI. Then why don't you ... sleep with me?

NOBU. By the time I get home from work I'm tired. Shig all day long, ordering me around, do this, do that. I even had to get up at 5:00 this morning to pick up the produce 'cause his damn son-in-law is a lazy son-of-a-bitch, I'm tired, I'm tired, Masi.

MASI. What about those magazines?

NOBU. I'll throw 'em out, OK? First thing tomorrow I'll throw 'em in the trash and burn 'em. That make you feel better? *(Masi is hurt by his angry response.)* Masi? *(No response.)* Masi. You're pretty. You are. *(Memory ends. Masi withdraws into shadows. Kiyoko returns to Nobu with earrings on. Lights come up.)*

KIYOKO. *(Posing.)* Nobu-chan?

NOBU. "Suteki da nah." [Looks beautiful.] *(Kiyoko attempts to embrace Nobu. It's too uncomfortable for Nobu and he gently pushes her away. Kiyoko is quite embarrassed. From now on they speak in English again.)*

KIYOKO. How come you do that to me? *(No response.)* Don't you like it?

NOBU. I like it. But I don't like it, too. *(Dim to darkness.)*

Scene 9

Masi's apartment. 4-5 days later. Couch has rumpled blanket on it. Morning. Sadao is standing holding the door open for a surprised Marsha. Sadao is dressed only in pants and an undershirt. Marsha is holding a box of "manju" [Japanese pastry]. They have never met.

SADAO. Good morning.

MARSHA. Is my mother ... Is Mrs. Matsumoto here?

MASI. *(Off.)* Who is it?

SADAO. Come on in, please come in. *(Masi enters in a bath-*

robe with her hair tied up in a towel as if just washed.)

MASI. *(Momentarily caught off guard.)* Oh, hi Marsha. Come in.

MARSHA. *(Entering hesitantly.)* Hello Mom.

MASI. This is Sadao Nakasato. *(To Sadao.)* My eldest one, Marsha.

SADAO. Hello Marsha.

MARSHA. Hello. *(Awkward pause. Marsha remembers her package.)* Oh, I just thought I'd bring some "manju" by. *(Handing it to Masi.)* I didn't think it was that early. Next time I guess I'll call first.

SADAO. Hmm, love "manju." Some of my favorites. Especially the ones with the "kinako" on top. The brown powdery stuff?

MARSHA. I meant to drop it off last night but I called and no one was here.

MASI. Oh, we got in late from fishing.

SADAO. We caught the limit.

MASI. *(Looking at phone answering machine.)* I have to remember to turn this machine on.

SADAO. In fact, Masi caught more than me.

MASI. Teamwork. I catch them and Sadao takes them off the hook. Sit down and have breakfast with us. Sit, sit.

MARSHA. That's OK Mom.

MASI. It was so late last night I told Sadao to sleep on the couch. So he did. He said he would cook breakfast for me in the morning. Right over there on the couch. *(Masi and Sadao are nodding to each other in agreement. Marsha doesn't move.)*

SADAO. Waffles.

MASI. You sure you know how?

SADAO. I can make them, good ones. From scratch.

MASI. Sit down, sit down.

MARSHA. No, no Mom. I really should be going. I'm going to stop over at the house. To see Dad, too.

MASI. No wait, wait ... I have some fish for you. *(Masi wrapping up two packages of fish with newspaper. Marsha notices.)*

MARSHA. Mom, I don't want any fish.

MASI. *(Handing her a package.)* Then give it to Brad.

MARSHA. Mom, I'm not seeing him anymore.

MASI. Oh, then give it to Dad.

MARSHA. What do I tell him?

MASI. *(Momentary pause.)* Just give it to him. No use wasting it. He can eat fish morning, noon and night. *(Masi hustling Marsha towards the door.)*

SADAO. No waffles? They're low cholesterol.

MARSHA. Uh, no thanks. Nice to meet you Mr. Nakasato. *(Marsha pauses at door. They exchange glances.)* Bye, Mom. *(Marsha exits.)*

MASI. *(Calling after.)* Tell Daddy I'll bring his clothes by, that I've been busy. And tell him to put his old clothes in a pile where I can see it. Last time I couldn't find one of his underwear and he got mad at me. *(Closes door.)* It was under the icebox. *(As Sadao rambles on, Masi seems lost in her thoughts.)*

SADAO. *(Caught up in his cooking.)* Everything's low cholesterol. Except for the Cool Whip. But that doesn't count because that's optional. Where's the MSG? That's my secret. My daughter gets so mad at me, "Dad, you're a pharmacist, you should know better than to use MSG." She's a health food nut ... *(Sadao is bending down to look in a lower cabinet for the MSG. As he disappears Masi moves into a pool of light. Memory sequence: Nobu lit in pool of light.)*

NOBU. No, Masi, I said size 8, size 8 hooks.

MASI. You told me to buy size 6, not size 8. That's not what you told me.

NOBU. I get home from the store I expect you to ... Jesus Christ ... *(Starting to pace.)*

MASI. Nobu, Nobu, you didn't tell me to get size 8 hooks. You told me size ...

NOBU. *(Interrupts.)* I said size 8. I said size 8 hooks. *(Pause.)* This is my house. Masi? After I come home from that damn store — here ... This is *my* house. *(Silence.)*

MASI. *(Quietly.)* I'm sorry. I'm wrong. You said size 8 hooks. *(Nobu withdraws. Lights up. End of memory. Sadao gets up from behind the cabinet with the MSG.)*

SADAO. You don't mind, do you? Masi? The "ajinomoto." Is it OK with you?

MASI. Yes, yes, it's fine. *(Sadao is aware of Masi's pensiveness.)*

SADAO. Sometimes I add prune juice but then you have to go easy on the MSG. The prune juice really does add a nice hint of flavor to the waffles if you don't overdo it. *(Nobu lit in half light looking at his unfinished kite frame.)* Everything in moderation. I think these people got a little carried away with this MSG thing. Of course, I'm not running a Chinese restaurant, either. I'm just talking about a tiny pinch of the stuff ... *(As lights go to half on Sadao and Masi, Nobu is lit in a pool of light. He lifts the kite above his head and begins to move it as if it were flying. For a moment Nobu appears like a child making believe his kite is soaring high above in the clouds. Nobu goes to half light.)*

Scene 10

Neighborhood streets. Kiyoko and Chiyo enter checking the addresses on houses.

CHIYO. Kiyoko, what's the address? What's the number?
KIYOKO. *(Looking at a piece of paper.)* 2158 "A" Street.
CHIYO. *(Looking.)* 2152, 2154 ... There it is. *(Judy hurries in, wiping her hands.)*
JUDY. Just a minute, I'm coming! *(Judy stops when she sees the two strangers at her door.)* Yes?
KIYOKO. I am a friend of your father. My name is Kiyoko Hasegawa.
CHIYO. Chiyo Froelich.
JUDY. Hi.
KIYOKO. I run a restaurant. "Hasegawas?"
CHIYO. Chiyo's Hair Salon, right next door.
JUDY. Oh.... Yeah, yeah.
KIYOKO. We are having a small get together at my place for your father.
CHIYO. A birthday party. *(They hear the baby crying.)*
KIYOKO. Oh, that must be Timothy.
CHIYO. Nobu should see him. *(Awkward pause.)*
JUDY. *(Starting to withdraw.)* I really should.... Excuse me ...

CHIYO. *(To Kiyoko.)* Show Judy your earrings. Kiyoko, show her.

KIYOKO. Chiyo.

CHIYO. He gave them to her. Your father. For her birthday.

KIYOKO. For my birthday. He comes to my restaurant almost every day. He likes my cooking. That's how come I know him so good.

CHIYO. *(Kidding.)* He's so "mendokusai" [troublesome]. I don't like cucumber pickle, I like eggplant. "Monku, monku" all the time.

KIYOKO. Oh, it's no trouble at all. I like to do things like that. I like to cook for Nobu. *(Timothy starts to cry in the back.)*

JUDY. *(Starting to leave.)* I really need to get back to the baby ...

KIYOKO. So can you come?

CHIYO. To the birthday?

JUDY. *(Exiting.)* I'm not sure. I'm really busy these days. Nice meeting you. *(Dim to darkness. Lights up on Nobu with his kite. Masi in half light moves away from Sadao. She's holding the fishing pole.)*

Scene 11

Nobu puts down the kite frame. Thinking. Picks up the phone and dials Masi's place. Masi's place in half light. Sadao at the counter making waffles. He hears the phone machine click on but does not answer it. Masi is off to the side studying her rod and reel.

NOBU. Masi? You got any ... Masi? *(Masi's phone machine kicks in. Nobu doesn't know how to deal with it.)*

MASI'S RECORDED VOICE. Hello. This is Masi Matsumoto. I'm not in right now, so please wait for the tone and leave your name, your number and a short message. Thank you, bye bye. *(Nobu listening to the message end. The beep sounds. He's panicked. Not quite sure what to do.)*

NOBU. I am Nobu Matsumoto. My telephone number is 751

... damn. *(Checks the number.)* 751-8263. *(Not sure if he has said his name.)* I am Nobu Matsumoto. *(Nobu hangs up. Picks up his kite and stares at it. Masi lit in pool of light. Casting. She is working on perfecting her technique, putting together all the little things that Sadao has taught her. She goes through one complete cycle without a hitch. Very smooth. Having done the whole thing without a mistake gives her great satisfaction. She smiles to herself. It feels good. She begins again. Dim to darkness on Masi and Nobu.)*

END OF ACT ONE

ACT TWO

Scene 1

Kiyoko's restaurant. 4 weeks later. Surprise birthday party for Nobu. Judy standing by herself out front, picking on the food. Curley and Marsha in the kitchen and Kiyoko and Chiyo scurrying about with last minute preparations. Over the restaurant speakers we hear a 40's tune like, "String of Pearls."*

KIYOKO. *(Calling.)* Curley! Hurry up with the "chicken teri!" *(Checking the food items.)* Ara! I forgot the dip. Chiyo, go talk, go talk. *(Kiyoko pushes Chiyo towards Judy, then hurries back into the kitchen as Curley and Marsha enter, carrying more food. Marsha is holding her nose.)*

CHIYO. *(To Judy, in passing.)* Nobu's favorite song. *(Stops momentarily, touching Judy's hair.)* You come see me, I know what to do with it. *(Chiyo heads back to the kitchen as Marsha and Curley are setting their dishes down.)*

CURLEY. If you think this stink, wait 'til you try my famous, "hom-yu."

MARSHA. *(Attempting to be polite.)* No, really, it wasn't that bad.

CURLEY. All orientals gotta have stink food. It's part of our culture. Chinese, Japanese, Koreans, Philippinos — We all got one dish that is so stink. Philippinos got fish gut paste, "bagaoong," Koreans, "kim chee." Whew! Chinese got this thing called, "ham-ha," shrimp paste. My mudda used to cook with it. Whew! Stink like something went die. *(Chiyo enters.)*

CHIYO. *(Admonishing.)* Curley.

CURLEY. *(Ignoring Chiyo.)* And us Buddhaheads eat "takuan," the pickled horse radish. When you open up the bottle, the neighbors call to see if your toilet went explode!

---

*   See Special Note on copyright page.

CHIYO. *(Poking head into the kitchen.)* Kiyoko! He's at it again!

CURLEY. Next time you come I make you my "hom-yu."

JUDY. Hom-yu? *(To Marsha.)* You know "hom-yu?"

MARSHA. It's some kind of vegetable dish or something? ...

CURLEY. No, no, no.... What's-a-matta? You guys live on Mars? You never heard of hom-yu? Hom-yu. Steamed pork hash. It's my specialty. Gotta have the stinky fish on top. That's the secret. Lottsa "Pake" [Chinese] places don't use that fish anymore. Know why? Too stink! Chase all the "haole" [white] customers away. Take pork butt, chop it into small pieces. Little pig snout, huh? Throw it in. Tastes so "ono." 4 water chestnuts, chopped. Teaspoon of cornstarch — *(Kiyoko entering with dip, Chiyo trailing.)*

KIYOKO. *(Interrupts.)* Curley! Curley! Go do the cake!

MARSHA. *(To Curley.)* I'll help you.

CHIYO. Kiyoko, when is he coming?

KIYOKO. *(To Chiyo.)* He should be on his way ... *(To Marsha.)* You shouldn't help anymore. Eat, eat. Talk to Chiyo. *(Continuing.)*

MARSHA. *(Overlapping.)* We met already ...

KIYOKO. *(Continuing. To Curley.)* Go, go, put the candles on the cake. No beer, either.

CURLEY. *(Exiting. Calling back to Marsha while scratching his butt.)* Stinky fish. Don't forget the stinky fish ...

KIYOKO. *(Following him out.)* Don't scratch your ... *(Kiyoko remembers the guests. As Kiyoko and Curley exit, Chiyo approaches Judy and Marsha.)*

CHIYO. I've never seen her like this. She's acting like a kid back there. *(Catching her breath and looking the two daughters over.)* You're Judy, neh, the 5th grade teacher?

JUDY. I am the 5th grade teacher.

CHIYO. And you're the dental — *(Continuing.)*

MARSHA. *(Overlapping.)* ... Hygienist, I told you earlier ...

CHIYO. *(Continuing.)* — hygienist — yeah, yeah you told me before. *(Quietly laughing about her mistake. Calms down.)* So. What do you think of the both of them? Nobu and Kiyoko? *(Awkward pause.)*

MARSHA. I think it's ... good. I think it's good. *(Chiyo looks to Judy who is silent.)*

CHIYO. *(Touching Judy's hair gently.)* You come see me. I know what to do with it. *(Chiyo turns and walks back towards the kitchen.)*

MARSHA. Judy.

JUDY. This is stupid — What am I doing here?

MARSHA. We're doing this for Dad.

JUDY. You really think he's going to want us here?

MARSHA. Judy ...

JUDY. Do you? *(Kiyoko hurries in, followed by Chiyo.)*

KIYOKO. Curley called — Nobu's not home, so he's coming. *(To Marsha, feigning enthusiasm.)* I'm so glad you could make it. Judy said you weren't sure whether you could all come or not.

MARSHA. Oh no, no. We wouldn't have missed it.

KIYOKO. Nobu-chan will be so happy you are here.

MARSHA. It was very kind of you to invite us.

KIYOKO. Oh, no, no, no. I wanted all of you here.

CHIYO. Yeah, yeah, we wanted all of you here.

KIYOKO. *(To Judy.)* Where is the baby?

JUDY. Jimmy's home babysitting him.

CHIYO. Next time you bring him. We got plenty of room here.

KIYOKO. Yes, please, please. Next time you bring the baby and Jimmy, too. I want to get to know all of Nobu-chan's family. *(Curley rushes in with his ukelele.)*

CURLEY. "HAYO! HAYO!" [Hurry! Hurry!] THE BUGGA'S COMING! THE BUGGA'S COMING!

CHIYO. I'll get the cake. Hide! Hide!

CURLEY. I got the lights.

KIYOKO. *(To Marsha and Judy.)* In here, in here ... *(Darkness. Nobu enters cautiously.)*

NOBU. Kiyoko! Kiyoko! *(The lights come up abruptly, then begin a slow fade through the rest of the scene.)*

ALL: SURPRISE! *(Nobu is first happy. Then he sees Judy and Marsha. He is in shock. Chiyo and Curley lead everyone in a rousing celebratory birthday song as Kiyoko enters with a birthday cake decorated with burning candles. He is attempting to appear happy, but he is becoming more and more upset that his daughters are there. Lights continue their slow fade through the song which is beginning to fall apart. Kiyoko is now standing next to Nobu holding the cake out in front of him. She senses something is wrong. The song ends with Curley and Kiyoko mumbling the last few lyrics. Silence. Nobu's face is illuminated by the glowing candles. Nobu makes no move to blow out the candles. The moment is now uncomfortable. Kiyoko is very upset.)*

KIYOKO. Nobu-chan, please.

JUDY. *(Irritated.)* Dad. *(Nobu still refuses to blow out the candles. Moment is now extremely awkward. No one knows what to do.)*

MARSHA. *(Gently.)* Daddy. *(Slowly Nobu leans forward and with a forceful breath extinguishes the candles.)*

Scene 2

Masi's place. Same night. Sadao and Masi on couch. Both are propped up, Sadao intently watching TV and Masi peering at the TV over the magazine she holds in front of her. Sadao keeps switching the channel with his remote control. Each time Masi starts to settle into a program, Sadao switches the channel causing her to jerk her head from the shock.

MASI. Sadao? *(Busy switching channels.)* Sadao?

SADAO. Hmm?

MASI. Could you please keep it on one?

SADAO. *(Realizing what he's been doing.)* Oh. I'm sorry. *(Starts switching channels again.)* Which one? This one? How's this?

MASI. Fine, fine. That's fine. *(They settle into watching TV.)* Sadao?

SADAO. Hmm?

MASI. I don't feel good. *(Pause.)* I think something's wrong with me.

SADAO. What, what? Want me to call Doc Tanaka?

MASI. No, no ...

SADAO. You have a fever? Headache? What's wrong?

MASI. No, no, nothing like that. *(Pause. Thinking.)* I'm too happy.

SADAO. What?

MASI. I feel ... too happy. *(Sadao stares at her uncomprehending.)* I used to feel like this as a kid, I think. But it was ... different. *(Pause.)*

SADAO. You feel too happy?

MASI. When you're a kid you get ice cream and 'member how you used to feel? Happy, right? But then you eat it all up and it's gone, or, you eat too much of it and you throw-up. But this just goes on and on.

SADAO. You mean us? *(Masi nodding.)* Yeah, but this is a little different than ice cream, don't you ...

MASI. *(Interrupts.)* Of course, of course, Sadao.

SADAO. What about with Nobu? Didn't you go through this with him? *(Masi shakes her head.)* I mean in the beginning when you first met? When you got married?

MASI. No, it wasn't like that. *(Pause.)* I think something's wrong with me. You know how they say there's no such thing as an accident? That you really wanted it to happen and so it did? I don't think I ever really cared for Nobu. Not the way he cared for me. There was someone else who liked me in Camp. I liked him, too. I married Nobu. Something's wrong with me, huh? Now you make me feel too happy. I don't like it. It makes me ... unhappy. *(They both laugh. Sadao reaches out and places his hand on top of hers.)* Was she in a lot of pain? *(Sadao doesn't follow her comment.)* Your wife. Towards the end. In the hospital.

SADAO. *(Realizes she's talking about his first wife, Mary.)* She just slept all the time. No, not too much. After about 2 weeks she went into a coma and that was it. You can't tell. Cancer's like that. Mary was pretty lucky, I guess. *(Pause. Thinking.)* There's nothing wrong with you. Really, there isn't. *(Pause. Trying to decide whether to say something or not.)* You scare me. You know that? Sometimes you scare me half to death. I don't want to go through that again. I told myself, 'never, ever again.' Dead is better than feeling that kind of pain. But this ... this is ... I don't know.... To get a second chance.... *(Pause.)* There's nothing good about growing old. You spend most of your time taking medicine and going to the doctor so you won't die. The rest of the time you spend going to the funerals of your friends who did die, and they were taking the same medicine and seeing the same doctors so what's the use, anyway? Huh? *(Sarcastically.)* The golden years.... Look at us. Here we are. At our age. Not even married. Can you imagine what the kids are thinking?

MASI. We're not doing anything wrong.

SADAO. Of course, I know, I know.

MASI. We're not doing anything wrong, Sadao. We're not.

SADAO. I know. But when I really think about what we're doing ... it embarrasses the hell out of me! *(They look at each other, then suddenly burst out laughing. They gradually calm down.)*

MASI. I scare you half to death. And you ... you make me feel so good I feel awful. *(They look at each other for a moment, then slowly reach out and embrace. Dim to darkness.)*

Scene 3

Kiyoko's restaurant. 1 week later. Nobu is sitting at counter sipping sake and eating eggplant pickles. Curley is watching him from the service window. He comes out sipping on a beer.

CURLEY. *(Takes a big gulp.)* Know why I like to drink beer? Know why? *(As Nobu looks up, Curley answers his own question with a loud satisfying "burp.")* Ahh. I like to let things out. Makes me feel good. Don't like to keep things bottled up inside. Not good for you. Give you an ulcer. Cancer. Maybe you just blow up and disappear altogether, huh. *(Laughs at his own joke. Notices Nobu isn't laughing.)* That's the problem with you "kotonks." You buggas from the mainland all the time too serious. *(Nobu glances back towards the door.)* No worry, no worry. Kiyoko going be back soon. Chiyo's place — yak, yak, yak. Hey, you had lots of girlfriends when you was small kid time?

(Nobu shrugs.) Strong silent type, huh. Me? Lottsa wahines. All the time like to play with Curley. *(Mimicking the girls.)* "Curley, darling you're so cute ... you're so funny." ... But I not all the time cute. I not all the time funny. How come you all the time come around here and you still got one wife?

NOBU. We're separated.

CURLEY. So when you gonna get the divorce?

NOBU. No. *(Curley doesn't understand.)* No.

CURLEY. What about Kiyoko? *(No response. Nobu keeps drinking.)* I don't like you. I like you. I don't like you 'cause you make Kiyoko feel lousy. I like you 'cause you make her happy. Hey, she's my boss — who you think catch hell if she not feeling good? Hey, I don't like catching hell for what you do ...

NOBU. *(Interrupts.)* It's none of your business — Kiyoko and me.

CURLEY None of my business? Hey, brudda, Kiyoko may be feeding your face but I'm the guy who's cooking the meals. *(Nobu stares down at his pickles.)* Nobu?

NOBU. What?

CURLEY. You like Kiyoko? *(No response.)* Well, do you?

NOBU. *(Under his breath.)* Yeah, I guess so.

CURLEY. 'Yeah, I guess so' what?

NOBU. *(Mumbling.)* I like Kiyoko.

CURLEY. Jesus. Talking to you "kotonks" is like pulling teeth.

NOBU. I LIKE KIYOKO! *(Pause.)* I like Kiyoko. *(Curley leans forward towards Nobu and "burps" loudly.)*

CURLEY. Feels good, huh? *(Nobu is disgusted. Curley smiles. Dim to darkness.)*

Scene 4

Nobu's place. 1 week later. Masi enters carrying the wash in a brown paper bag. She unpiles the clothes and stacks them neatly on the kitchen table. She picks up the old clothes off the floor, folds them and puts them in the bag. As she looks up, one gets the sense that she is trying to decide whether to say hello to Nobu or just leave. She looks for a moment towards the hallway, then decides otherwise. Just as she turns and starts to make her way towards the door with the bag, Nobu enters from the hallway.

NOBU. Masi, is that you? *(Nobu realizes that she's leaving without bothering to say hello. Masi senses this and feels guilty.)*
MASI. I was going. I'm a little late. I was just going to leave the clothes and go. *(As she speaks, she notices the dirty dishes on the coffee table. She puts down the bag and proceeds to clean up the mess as she continues to talk.)* I didn't know you were in the back ... *(Masi points to the dishes in the sink. Nobu just watches.)* Nobu, why don't you wash the dishes once in a while? Clean up.
NOBU. Place is a dump anyway. *(Masi stops and looks at him. Nobu presses the point.)* Place is a dump, Mama. Neighborhood's no good. Full of colored people. Mexicans ...
MASI. *(Putting dishes in sink.)* Well, move then. Move to the north side like me. I kept saying that all along. For the kids — better schools, better neighborhood.... Think you listen to me? *(Mimicking Nobu.)* I don't like "Hakujin" — white people make me nervous. So you don't like white people, you don't like black people, you don't like Mexicans.... So who do you like? Huh? "Monku, monku, monku" [kvetch, kvetch, kvetch].
NOBU. *(Muttering.)* I don't mind Mexicans. *(Pause.)* I told Shig you can't keep stocking all that Japanese things when the "Nihonjins" [Japanese] are moving out of the neighborhood. You gotta sell to the Mexicans and not all that cheap crap, too, 'cause they can tell. Think Shig listens to me? He's the big store owner. The big man. If I was running the store it woulda been different. Different. *(Pause.)* And your old man said he'd get me that store.
MASI. It wasn't his fault. He didn't plan on the war, Nobu.
NOBU. He promised he could set me ... *(Continuing.)*
MASI. *(Overlapping.)* It wasn't his fault.
NOBU. *(Continuing.)* ... up in business or anything else I wanted to do.
MASI. IT WASN'T HIS FAULT! *(Silence.)* Who wanted to be

in the Relocation Camps. Did you? Do you think he wanted to be in there. It broke Papa's heart. He spent his entire life building up that farm. Papa was a proud man. A very proud man. It broke his heart when he lost it. And how come you didn't go to the bank like I told you. I told you to go to the bank and ask for ...

NOBU. I'm just saying I'd run the business different. Shig is a "baka" [fool]. That's all I'm saying.

MASI. You're retired. Shig passed away 8 years ago. The store's not even ... *(Continuing.)*

NOBU. *(Overlapping.)* If all the Japanese move out you can't keep selling all that Japanese things, you can't. That's all I'm saying.

MASI. *(Continuing.)* ... there anymore. It's a cleaners. *(Silence. Masi picks up the paper bag of old clothes and starts to move towards the door. She's had enough.)*

NOBU. Masi?

MASI. *(Stops.)* What?

NOBU. Mr. Rossi give you anymore fish?

MASI. *(Uncomfortable lying.)* No. Not lately. *(Pause.)*

NOBU. Mama?

MASI. Is your back bothering you, Nobu? *(No response.)* Want me to "momo" [massage] it for you? *(Nobu nods. As Masi moves to put the bag down, Nobu removes his undershirt so he is bare chested. He seats himself. Masi begins to massage his shoulders from behind. They continue in silence. Nobu is enjoying the moment. He begins to quietly laugh to himself.)* What?

NOBU. When I started work at your Papa's farm, he wanted to put me in the packing shed. I said "No, I want to work in the fields." It was so hot, 110 degrees out there. He thought I was nuts. But I knew everyday at 8 in the morning and 12 noon you and your sister would bring the water out to us.

MASI. *(Laughing as she recalls.)* Nobu.

NOBU. I wanted to watch you.

MASI. You would just stand there with your cup, staring at me.

NOBU. Hell, I didn't know what to say.

MASI. You drank so much water, Lila and I thought maybe

39

you had rabies. We used to call you, "Nobu, the Mad Dog."
(Both laughing.) Papa liked you.

NOBU. Boy, he was a tough son-of-a-bitch.

MASI. I didn't think anyone could keep up with Papa. But,
you could work like a horse. You and Papa. Proud. Stubborn.
(Masi massages Nobu in silence.)

NOBU. Masi? Why don't you cook me breakfast?

MASI. What?

NOBU. Cook me breakfast. I miss my hot rice and raw egg
in the morning.

MASI. It's late Nobu. You have your wash. I'm not going to
come all the way back over here just to cook you ...

NOBU. *(Interrupts.)* Just breakfast. Then in the morning when
we get up you can go back to your place. *(Masi stops, realizing he is asking her to spend the night. Masi does not move. Nobu
stares ahead. More silence. Then, tentatively, she moves her hands
forward and begins to massage him. A faint smile appears on Nobu's
face. Dim to darkness.)*

Scene 5

*Kiyoko's restaurant. 1 week later. Curley, after hours, seated
in semi-darkness. Feet up on table, accompanying himself on
the ukelele and singing a sad, Hawaiian folk song like
"Manuela Boy."* As he sings, Masi's place is lit in a pool
of light. Sadao stands before the door Masi has just opened.
In Sadao's right hand he holds a suitcase and in his left
several fishing poles. On his head sits a fishing hat. Sadao
has come to move in with Masi. For a moment they look at
each other in silence. Then Masi invites him in. Sadao enters. Dim to darkness. Finishing song, dim to darkness on
Curley.)*

*   See Special Music Note on copyright page.

Scene 6

Nobu's place. 3 days later. Late afternoon. Judy has stopped by with Timothy. Judy sets the baby down on the kitchen table U. of Nobu. Nobu turns to look at Judy, then returns to working on the kite and watching TV. This is the first time Judy has visited Nobu since their break up over her marriage. He has never seen Timothy.

JUDY. *(Moving down towards Nobu.)* I was just driving by and I thought I'd stop in. *(No response.)* You doing OK, Dad? *(Silence.)* You know, Mom? I just wanted to say ...

NOBU. *(Interrupts.)* Did he come?

JUDY. *(Exasperated.)* No, he did not.

NOBU. He can come to the house now.

JUDY. 'He can come to the house now'? Jesus Christ Dad, he isn't one of your children. He doesn't need your permission. He's ... *(Continuing.)*

NOBU. *(Overlapping.)* This is my house. He needs my permission.

JUDY. *(Continuing.)* ... grown man. I don't want to fight. I didn't come here to fight with you Dad.

NOBU. I *said* he can come ...

JUDY. *(Interrupts.)* He won't come, he doesn't like you! *(Silence.)*

NOBU. Damn "kurochan" ...

JUDY. He's black, not "kurochan." It's African American. *(Pause.)* Everybody marries out, OK? Sanseis don't like sanseis.

NOBU. Tak's son married a "Nihonjin," Shig's daughter did, your cousin Patsy ... *(Continuing.)*

JUDY. *(Overlapping.)* OK, OK, I didn't, alright.

NOBU. *(Continuing.)* ... did, Marsha's going to. *(Pause. Looking back to Timothy.)*

JUDY. But is that any reason not to see my baby? He's a part of you, too.

NOBU. No, no. Japanese marry other Japanese, their kids are "yonsei" [4th generation Japanese American] — not these damn "ainoko" [biracial person]. *(Silence.)*

JUDY. You're gonna to die out, you know that. You're gonna be extinct and nobody's gonna give a goddamn. *(Timothy has begun to cry softly. She goes over and picks the baby up, trying to soothe him. Judy, composing herself, decides to try one last time to say what she came to tell her father. Judy walks back to Nobu, this time carrying Timothy with her.)* Dad? *(No response.)* Daddy, you know Mom's moving out of the house? I didn't put her up to it. Honest. *(Silence. Nobu stares straight ahead. Beginning to cry.)* If I did ... I'm sorry.

NOBU. Judy ... *(More silence from Nobu. Judy gives up trying to talk to this man. As she turns to leave, she notices Nobu. He is looking towards her, at Timothy. Something in his expression makes Judy bring the baby over to Nobu.)*

JUDY. *(Holding the baby out.)* Timothy. Your grandson. *(For a moment there is hesitation. We are not sure whether Nobu is going to take the baby. Then, Nobu reaches out and takes Timothy. Judy watches as Nobu awkwardly holds his grandson for the first time. As Judy begins to withdraw from the scene U. into a pool of light, Marsha is also lit U. in her own separate pool of light. Nobu remains lit holding Timothy. He begins to hum the traditional Japanese lullaby, "Donguri." Marsha and Judy watch Nobu and Timothy as they speak.)*

MARSHA. You didn't tell Dad, did you?

JUDY. No. I just brought the baby by.

MARSHA. It's going to kill him when he finds out.

JUDY. He's got that other woman.

MARSHA. Judy. *(Pause.)* Maybe he already knows about Mom and Mr. Nakasato.

JUDY. I don't think so. I really don't think so. *(They continue to watch as Nobu begins to sing the "Donguri" song to Timothy.)*

NOBU. *(Singing.)*

Donguri koro koro, donguri ko
Oike ni hamatte, saa taihen
Dojō ga dette kite, 'konnichiwa'
Timothy isshoni, asobimashō ...

42

Donguri koro koro, donguri ko
Oike ni hamatte, saa taihen
Dojō ga dette kite, 'konnichiwa'
Timothy isshoni, asobimashō ...
[Translation:
Acorn, acorn, rolling along
Fell into a pond, what will we do?
Up comes a loache fish, says 'good afternoon.
Timothy, let's go play together.]
(*Marsha and Judy dim to darkness first. Nobu is left alone in a pool of light singing to Timothy. As he dims to darkness, we hear the whir of a coffee grinder.*)

Scene 7

Masi's place. 2 days later. Masi has asked Judy and Marsha over for a talk. She has just told them she is going over to see Nobu. She is going to tell him that she wants a divorce and to marry again.

The two daughters sit uneasily while Masi is at the counter preparing coffee. Masi is trying to get the Braun grinder to work. She's getting the feel of it by pushing the button. We hear the whir of the spinning rotor blade.

She's ready. Takes the plastic top off and pours the beans in. Then, presses the start button. Just as the grinder picks up top speed Masi accidentally pulls the plastic top off. Beans go flying every which way! Pelting her face, bouncing off the cabinets. Quiet. Masi peeks from behind her hands. A couple of beans embedded in her hair fall to the counter. Masi is upset. The daughters are embarrassed. Normally, this would be a funny situation for them.

Marsha starts to pick up the beans scattered on the floor. Judy starts to giggle — it's all too ridiculous.

JUDY. *(Trying to suppress her laughter.)* I'm sorry, I'm sorry ...

MARSHA. I'll clean it up. *(Masi begins to laugh.)*

JUDY. God, what a mess.

MASI. *(To Marsha.)* Let it go, don't bother. I'll take care of it later. *(Judy finds a man's sock.)*

JUDY. *(Teasing.)* What's this? This belong to Mr. Nakasato?

MASI. *(Grabbing it.)* Judy.

MARSHA. Why didn't you just leave sooner? You didn't have to stick around for us.

MASI. I didn't. I was ... I was scared.

MARSHA. Of Dad?

MASI. I don't know. Everything.

JUDY. Was it 'cause I kept harping on you to move out on him all those years? Is that why you left?

MARSHA. What's the difference now?

JUDY. Marsha. *(Pause.)*

MASI. There are things you kids don't know. I didn't want to talk about them to you but ... Daddy and I, we didn't sleep ... *(Continuing.)*

JUDY. *(Overlapping.)* That's OK, Mom. Really, it's OK ...

MASI. *(Continuing.)* ... together. Every time I wanted to, he would push me away. Ten, fifteen years he didn't want me. *(Pause.)* We were having one of our arguments, just like always. And he was going on and on about how it was my fault this and my fault that. And I was trying to explain my side of it, when he turned on me, 'Shut up Mama. You don't know anything. You're stupid.' Stupid. After 42 years of letting him be right he called me that. And I understood. He didn't even need me to make him be right anymore. He just needed me to be stupid. I was tired. I couldn't fight him anymore. He won. He finally made me feel like shit. *(Judy and Marsha are shocked by her strong language.)* That was the night I left him and came over to your place. *(Nodding towards Judy.)* I like Sadao. *(Turns to Marsha.)* I like Sadao very much. *(Marsha turns away, then gets up and exits. Masi sends Judy after Marsha to comfort her. Dim to darkness.)*

Scene 8

Nobu's place. Same day. A song like "String of Pearls"* can be heard playing faintly in the background. He's fixing himself in front of a small wall mirror. He adjusts the collar of his shirt and tugs at his sweater until it looks right. Nobu checks his watch. As he begins to pick up some of the scattered clothes on the floor, Masi enters. Music cue ends.

Nobu quickly gets up and moves to the sofa. Masi goes over to the kitchen area and takes clothes out of the bag setting them neatly on the table. She picks up the dirty clothes off the floor, folds them, and puts them into the bag. As she's doing this, Nobu gets up, shuffles over to the stove and turns on the flame to heat some water. Stands there and watches the water heat up.

MASI. *(Sits down on sofa.)* I want to talk, Nobu. *(No response. Nobu gets the tea out and pours some into the pot.)* I have something I want to tell you.

NOBU. *(Moving back to couch.)* Want some tea? *(As Nobu sits, Masi gets up and moves towards the sink area. She gets a sponge and wipes off the tea leaves he has spilled on the counter. Nobu turns the TV on and stares at it.)*

MASI. You know Dorothy and Henry's son, George?

NOBU. The pharmacist or something?

MASI. No, the lawyer one. He's the lawyer one. I went to see him. I went to see about a divorce. About getting one. *(No response.)* I want to get married again. So I went to George to see about a divorce. I wanted to tell you first so you'd know. I didn't want you to hear from someone else. I know how you hate that kind of thing. Thinking something's going on behind your back.

NOBU. Wait, wait, wait a second. You want to get.... What?

---

*   See Special Note on copyright page.

What's all this?

MASI. It's the best thing, Nobu. We've been separated how long now? How long have we been living different places?

NOBU. I don't know. I never thought about it. Not too long.

MASI. 13 months.

NOBU. 13 months, who cares? I never thought about it.

MASI. It's the same as being divorced isn't it?

NOBU. It doesn't seem that long. You moved out of this house. It wasn't my idea. It was your idea. I never liked it.

MASI. It doesn't matter whose idea it was. It's been over a year since we ...

NOBU. *(Interrupts.)* You want to get married? Yeah, I know it's been over a year but I always thought.... You know that we'd ...

MASI. *(Interrupts.)* It's been over a year, Nobu.

NOBU. I know! I said I know. *(Pause.)*

MASI. I've been seeing someone. It wasn't planned or anything. It just happened.

NOBU. What do you mean, 'seeing someone?' What do you mean?

MASI. He's very nice. A widower. He takes me fishing. He has a nice vegetable garden that he ...

NOBU. *(Interrupts.)* Who is he? Do I know him? Is it someone I know?

MASI. His name is Sadao Nakasato. His wife died about 2 years ago. He's related to Dorothy and Henry. Nobu, it's the best thing for both of us.

NOBU. You keep saying it's the best thing, the best thing. *(Pause.)* Masi, why did you sleep with me that night? *(Silence.)*

MASI. Aren't you seeing somebody?

NOBU. No. Not like that.

MASI. But the kids said she's very nice. That she invited ...

NOBU. *(Interrupts.)* It's totally different! I'm not seeing anyone! *(Pause.)* How long have you been seeing this guy? How long?

MASI. Please, Nobu. You always get what *you* want. I always let you have your way. For once just let ...

NOBU. *(Interrupts.)* HOW LONG!

MASI. About 5 months.

NOBU. 5 MONTHS! How come you never told me? Do the girls know, too? The girls know! Everybody knows? 5 months. 5 GODDAMN MONTHS AND I DON'T KNOW!! *(Nobu breaks the kite.)*

MASI. I asked them not to tell you.

NOBU. Why? Why the hell not? Don't I have a right to know??

MASI. Because I knew you'd react this way. Just like this. Yelling and screaming just like you always do.

NOBU. Everybody in this whole goddamn town knows except me! How could you do this to me! Masi! HOW COULD YOU DO THIS TO ME?? *(Nobu has her by the shoulders and is shaking her violently.)*

MASI. Are you going to hit me? *(Pause. Nobu slowly composes himself and lets her go.)* Because I want to be happy, Nobu. I want to be happy. *(Masi exits. Nobu left standing alone. Dim to darkness.)*

Scene 9

Kiyoko's restaurant. Same day, evening. Chiyo and Kiyoko seated at table. Lit in pool of light.

KIYOKO. 9 years. That's how long it has been. 9 years since Harry passed away. He never treated me like this. I call, I go over there. Harry never treated me like this.

CHIYO. Kiyoko. Maybe you have to stop thinking about Nobu. Hmm? Maybe ... maybe you should give him up. *(Silence.)* Kiyoko. Lots more fish in the ocean. Lots more. Go out with us. Come on.

KIYOKO. I don't do those kinds of things.

CHIYO. I'll introduce you to some new guys. Remember Ray — you met him? I've been telling him about —

KIYOKO. *(Interrupts.)* I don't do those kinds of things. *(Pause.)* It's not easy for me, Chiyo. *(Silence.)* When Harry died, right after? I started taking the bus to work. I had a car, I could drive. It was easier to drive. I took the bus. For 25 years you go to sleep with him, wake up next to him. He shaves while you shower, comes in from the yard all sweaty. Then he's gone. No more Harry in bed. No more smell of aftershave in the towel you're drying off with. No more sweaty Harry coming up and hugging me. I had a car. I took the bus. I missed men's smells. I missed the smell of men. Every morning I would get up and walk to the corner to take the bus. It would be full of all these men going to work. And it would be full of all these men coming home from work. I would sit there pretending to read my magazine ... *(Inhales. Discovering the different smells.)* Soap ... just washed skin ... aftershave lotion ... sweat ... *(Lights come up to half in the restaurant. Curley bursts through the kitchen doors holding a plate of his famous "Hom-yu." Brings it over and sets it down on the table which is now lit in a full pool of light.)*

CURLEY. Hom-yu! Hom-yu!

CHIYO. Curley, kusai yo!

CURLEY. I know stink but stink GOOD!

KIYOKO. Curley!

CURLEY. *(Motioning.)* Hayo, hayo — all dis good food back dere going to waste. Gonna need a gas mask for all da stinky stuff back dere. Come on, come on, I been cooking all day. Hayo, hayo, kau kau time ... *(As lights dim, Curley ushers Kiyoko and Chiyo off stage into the kitchen.)*

Scene 10

Nobu's place. 2 days later. Knock at the door and Marsha enters carrying a brown paper bag. Nobu is watching TV.

MARSHA. Mom asked me to drop these by and to pick up the dirty clothes. *(No response. Marsha unpacks the newly washed clothes.)* Kiyoko's been calling me. She's worried about you. She says you won't see anybody. Why don't you just talk to her Dad?

NOBU. How come you didn't tell me? All the time you come here and you never mention it once. You. I feel so goddamned ashamed. All the time right under my nose. Everyone laughing at me behind my ...

MARSHA. *(Interrupts.)* Dad, Dad, it's not like that at all. I just didn't think it was all that important to tell ...

NOBU. *(Interrupts.)* Oh, come on! Mom told you not to tell me so she could go sneaking 'round with that son-of-a-bitch!

MARSHA. Alright, alright, but it's not like that at all. No one's trying to hide anything from you and no one's laughing at you.

NOBU. *(Moving her towards the couch and pushing her down while speaking.)* Sit down, sit down over here. Who is he? What does he do? Tell me 'bout him! Tell me!

MARSHA. *(Seated.)* What do you want me to say? Huh, Dad? They're happy. He's a nice man.

NOBU. *(Repeating.)* 'He's a nice man.' What the hell's that supposed to mean?

MARSHA. He treats her like a very special person.

NOBU. Well everyone does that in the beginning. In the beginning it's so easy to be ...

MARSHA. *(Interrupts.)* She laughs. All the time she's laughing. They're like two little kids. They hold hands. Did you ever do that? I'm embarrassed to be around them. He takes her fishing. He has a little camper and they drive up to Lake Berryessa and camp over night ... *(Continues right through.)*

NOBU. Alright, alright ...

MARSHA. *(Continuing.)* ... He teaches her how to bait the hook and cast it out.

NOBU. *(Overlapping.)* She doesn't like fishing.

MARSHA. *(Continuing.)* I mean you never even took her fishing.

NOBU. I tried to take her lots of times, she wouldn't go.

MARSHA. *(Continuing.)* They even dig up worms in his garden at his house. I saw them. Side by side. *(Continuing.)*

NOBU. Alright, I said.

MARSHA. *(Continuing.)* ... sitting on the ground digging up worms and ... *(Continuing.)*

NOBU. *(Overlapping.)* ALRIGHT! ALRIGHT!

MARSHA. *(Continuing.)* ... putting them in a coffee can! I MEAN DID YOU EVER DO THAT FOR MOM!! *(Pause. Quieter.)* Did you? *(Getting worked up again.)* You're so ... so stupid. You are. You're stupid. All you had to say was 'come back.' 'Please come back.' You didn't even have to say, 'I'm sorry.' *(Continuing.)*

NOBU. *(Overlapping.)* I'm your father ...

MARSHA. *(Continuing.)* ... Mom would've come back. She would've. That's all you had to say. 3 lousy words: 'Please come back.' *(Continuing.)*

NOBU. *(Overlapping.)* I'm your father ...

MARSHA. *(Continuing.)* ... You ruined everything. It's all too late! YOU WRECKED EVERYTHING! *(Pause. Composing herself.)* I'm so mixed up. When I look at Mom I'm happy for her. When I think about you ... I don't know. You have Kiyoko.

NOBU. That's not the same. I'm talking about your Mama.

MARSHA. Dad, Kiyoko cares a great deal about you. She's been calling Judy and me day and night.

NOBU. She knocks on the door but I don't let her in. She's not Mama.

MARSHA. Dad. What do you want me to say? That's the way it is. I used to keep thinking you two would get back together. I couldn't imagine life any other way. But slowly I just got used to it. Mom over there and you here. Then all this happened. I mean, sometimes I can't recognize Mom anymore. What do you want me to say? You'll get used to it.

NOBU. *(Pause, upset. Then stubbornly.)* No. *(Marsha looks at her father sadly.)*

MARSHA. You'll get used to it. *(Dim to darkness on Marsha and Nobu.)*

Scene 11

Masi and Judy at the clothes line. Judy holding Timothy while Masi hangs clothes. An agitated Nobu enters and begins to pull Masi home.

JUDY. Dad ...

MASI. Nobu ...

NOBU. I won't yell Mama, I won't yell at you anymore. I won't "monku" about — *(Continuing.)*

MASI. *(Overlapping.)* Nobu? Nobu, what are you — *(Continuing.)*

JUDY. *(Overlapping.)* Dad, Dad ...

MASI. *(Continuing.)* — doing? Let go, Nobu ...

NOBU. *(Continuing.)* — the store or about your Papa — I won't "monku," I won't do any of that stuff —

MASI. Let go of my arm! *(Silence.)*

NOBU. I tried, I tried Masi. After the war, after we got out of Camp? After — *(Continuing.)*

MASI. *(Overlapping.)* Nobu, Camp? What are you —

NOBU. *(Continuing)* — we got out I went to the bank like you told me. So your Papa can't give me money, that's alright — *(Continuing.)*

MASI. *(Overlapping.)* Nobu, what's this — you never told me —

NOBU. *(Continuing.)* — I'll do it on my own. I got there and ask the man how do I sign up to get money. He says sit there and wait. I wait, I wait, I wait 5 whole goddamn hours. I go up, 'How come nobody sees me?' He says, 'Sorry, but the person to see you is sick, come back tomorrow.' I get so pissed off I throw the magazines all over the place. Everyone is looking. I don't give a damn, I'm shaking I'm so pissed off. And then, and then ... I'm filled with shame. Shame. Because I threw their magazines all over. After what they did to me, "I'm" ashamed, me, "me." When I get home I feel something getting so tight inside of me. In my guts, tighter and tighter, getting all balled up. How come I feel

51

like this? Huh? How come I feel like this? I'm scared, Masi.
I'm scared. Please. I need — *(Continuing.)*
MASI. *(Overlapping.)* You don't understand, you don't —
NOBU. *(Continuing.)* — you. I need you. "You." You know.
You understand how it is now. Please, please, you come home,
you come — *(Continuing. Nobu begins to pull Masi home.)*
MASI. *(Overlapping.)* Nobu, Nobu, I can't, I —
NOBU. *(Continuing.)* — home now, Mama. Just like always.
You come home — *(Continuing.)*
MASI. *(Overlapping.)* — can't Nobu.
NOBU. Just like always ...
MASI. I can't. *(Nobu begins to break down, letting go of Masi.
Begins to plead.)*
NOBU. I'm sorry, I'm sorry, Masi. It's no good, it's no good,
Masi. Please come home. Please come home. Please ... *(Judy
pulls Masi away and they withdraw from the scene. Nobu is left alone
in a pool of light. Slowly pulls himself upright, staring into the darkness. He turns and crosses back to his room. He reaches behind his
chair and pulls out a long, narrow object wrapped in cloth. As he
unwraps it, we see what it is. A shotgun. We hear the mournful wail
of a "shakuhachi" flute. Nobu sits down on the chair with the gun
across his lap. Dim to darkness on Nobu.)*

Scene 12

*Kiyoko's restaurant. Chiyo at the phone dialing Nobu's
number. A concerned Curley stands guard next to her.
Kiyoko has told them not to bother with him anymore. Kiyoko
appears and watches them. She makes no attempt to stop
them. Chiyo lets the phone ring. Nobu seated in his chair,
stares at the phone ringing next to him. He gets up, still
holding the gun and exits. No one is answering. Chiyo and
Curley exchange disappointed looks. Only then does Kiyoko
burst in on them.*

KIYOKO. How come you keep doing that? Huh? Don't

phone him anymore. I told you, didn't? *(Kiyoko exits.)*
CURLEY. *(To Chiyo.)* Hey, maybe it's none of our business.
(Dim to darkness on the restaurant.)

Scene 13

*Masi's place. 1 week later. Nobu standing inside with a
shotgun. Sadao asleep off stage in the bedroom.*

NOBU. Where is he? *(Masi stares at the gun.)*
MASI. He went to buy the newspaper.
NOBU. *(Notices Masi watching him cautiously.)* It's not loaded.
(Beat.) I thought about it all week, all week. Coming over
here, shooting the son-of-a-bitch. I coulda. I coulda done it.
(Pause.) I just wanted to show you. Both of you. That's why I
brought it. Don't worry. It's not loaded. *(Nobu cracks the gun
and shows her that it is not loaded.)* I just wanted to show both
of you how it was, how I was feeling. But it's alright. You two.
It's alright now. *(Nobu sets the gun against the wall. Masi watches
him, trying to decide if it is indeed safe.)*
MASI. Nobu.
NOBU. Yeah?
MASI. He's taking a nap. In the bedroom. He likes to do
that after dinner.
NOBU. What is he? An old man or something?
MASI. He just likes to take naps. You do, too.
NOBU. In front of the TV. But I don't go into the bedroom
and lie down. Well, where is he? Bring him out. Don't I get
to meet him?
MASI. You sure? *(Masi looks at him for a long while. She believes
him. She turns to go wake Sadao up, then stops.)* Chester
Yoshikawa? That night in the Camps when I didn't show up
for the dance? Chester Yoshikawa? We just talked. That's all.
*(Masi leaves for the bedroom to awaken Sadao. Nobu looks slowly
around the apartment. It's Masi and yet it isn't. Nobu suddenly has
no desire to meet Sadao. He doesn't want to see them together in this*

apartment. Nobu exits abruptly. Masi appears cautiously leading out a yawning Sadao. They looked around. No Nobu. All they see is his shotgun leaning against the wall.)

Scene 14

As Masi and Sadao dim to darkness, Marsha and Judy lit in a pool of light extreme D. Marsha is holding a small kite and slowly moving it above Timothy who is held by Judy. They sit in silence as Marsha moves the kite.

JUDY. I can't believe he gave the kite to Timothy. He gets so mad if you even touch them. And he never flies them. *(Pause.)*
MARSHA. (*Moving the kite.*) No. He never flies them. *(They dim to half. They turn to watch the action taking place C.)*

Scene 15

Darkness. 2 days later. On stage, the TV light comes on. Nobu's face lit by the screen's light. Lights come up and Nobu is now lit in a pool of light, seated at sofa watching TV. No kite on the coffee table. The rest of place is in darkness. Masi is lit in a pool of light. She stands, staring pensively D. into space. In her arms she is holding the brown paper bag of newly washed clothes. She turns and moves towards Nobu's place. As she enters the lights come up full on the house.

Nobu is still sitting on the sofa watching TV. Masi goes over to the kitchen table and takes out the newly washed clothes, stacking them in neat piles on the table. She then proceeds to pick up the clothes scattered on the floor and to put them in the bag. She is ready to leave. Masi takes the bag of dirty clothes and moves towards the door, then stops. She makes up her mind about something she has been struggling with for a while. Masi returns to the kitchen and leaves the bag of Nobu's dirty clothes on the table. As she opens the door to leave, Masi looks back at Nobu and watches him for a brief moment.

During this whole time, Nobu has never turned around to look at Masi though he is very aware of what is going on. Masi sadly turns and exits through the door. Lights dim with Nobu silently watching TV. Briefly, Nobu's face is lit by the dancing light of the television screen. At the same instant, the brown paper bag of wash on the table is illuminated by a shaft of light. His phone begins to ring. Nobu turns to look at it. Black out on Nobu. The wash fades into darkness. The phone continues ring for a few moments. Then, silence.

END OF PLAY

PROPERTY LIST

ACT ONE

Scene 1
>Dirty clothes on table
>Pot of water with two hotdogs
>Wash rack with: 2 plates, 3 cups, 2 shallow bowls, chopsticks
>Rice bowl with cold rice (covered with plastic wrap)
>Teapot
>Tea
>French's Mustard jar (small)
>Lazy Susan with various condiments
>*San Jose Mercury* newspaper
>Kite frame, partially put together
>Kite kit (small box)
>inside: 3 brushes
>   2 jars
>   string
>   white glue
>Purse (Masi)
>Large bag with tomatoes and Japanese eggplant
>Reading glasses
>Large bag with clean, folded clothes

Scene 2
>Bottle of Budweiser beer (Curley)
>2 towels (Kiyoko, Curley)
>Teapot
>3 teacups
>Chopsticks
>Karaoke machine with 2 microphones
>Quarter (Nobu)
>Napkin holder
>Shoyu bottle

56

Scene 3
> Tray with 2 cups and saucers, 2 spoons, plate with
>> cookies, 2 cloth napkins, sugar, non-dairy creamer
> Sanka coffee jar
> Fishing pole with reel (in 2 pieces) (wrapped)
> 2 telephones (Nobu, Masi)

Scene 4
> Can of beer
> Six-pack of beer
> Stacked deck of cards
> Poker chips
> Green table cloth

Scene 5
> Casserole
> Small paper bag with fruit inside
> Tray
> 2 coffee cups, one with coffee, one with tea
> Bowl of olives, covered
> 2 napkins
> 1 large spoon
> 2 spoons
> Towel
> 2 throw pillows
> Pottery ash tray

Scene 7
> Clothesline, with clothes
> Clothespins
> Laundry hamper with clothes
> Baby wrapped in blanket
> Baby carrier

Scene 8
> Small gift box with earrings

Scene 9
> Blanket
> Pillow
> Manju in box
> Cooler
> Newspaper
> Fish
> Waffle ingredients
> Bowl
> Wisk
> Measuring cups and spoons
> Jar of MSG
> Kite #2 (almost finished)

Scene 10
> Piece of paper with address written on it (Kiyoko)
> Earrings (Kiyoko)
> Baby washcloth (Judy)

Scene 11
> Answering machine (Masi)
> Fishing pole (Masi)

ACT TWO

Scene 1
> Food: sushi, chicken teriyaki, dip (in bowl), manju
> (on plate), stinky fish (Alpo, in small bowl), oxtail
> stew (on plate), hash (small plate)
> Birthday cake with candles
> Paper plates
> Paper napkins
> Origami streamers
> Celery (Chiyo)
> Ukelele (Curley)

Scene 2
> Catalog (Masi)
> TV remote (Sadao)

Scene 3
> Sake bottle
> Sake cup
> Combo plate
> Chopsticks
> Napkin
> Bottle of beer
> Bar towel

Scene 4
> Brown paper bag with clean clothes
> Dirty clothes
> Dirty dishes
> Dishwashing liquid
> Sponge
> 1 cup
> Scissors
> Kite kit with glue and string
> Kite #3, almost done

Scene 5
> Ukelele
> 2 suitcases (Sadao)
> Tackle box

Scene 6
> Baby in baby carrier
> Tea cup (Nobu)

Scene 7
> Coffee grinder
> Coffee beans
> Man's Argyle sock

Scene 8

Wristwatch (Nobu)
Dirty clothes
Brown bag with clean clothes (Masi)
Teapot with tea
2 cups
Tray
Sponge
Dishwashing liquid

Scene 9

Homyu (steamed pork hash) (Curley)
2 beers (Chiyo, Kiyoko)

Scene 10

Brown bag with clean clothes (Marsha)
Dirty clothes

Scene 11

Clothesline with 2 pieces
Clothespins
Hamper with clothes (Judy)
Baby (Masi)
Shotgun (Nobu)

Scene 12

Telephone (Chiyo)

Scene 13

Shotgun (Nobu)

Scene 14

Small kite (Marsha)
Baby (Judy)

Scene 15

Brown bag with clean clothes
Dirty clothes

COSTUME LIST

Women

Masi

Navy-blue/green plaid cotton dress
Navy-blue pointelle sweater
Off-white/pink/blue paisley blouse (tie collar)
Plum dirndl skirt
Off-white/red/blue/green apron
Light grey/lavender flannel night gown
Purple chenille robe
Light-blue towel with Velcro tabs
Light-blue pinoir, gown and robe
Mauve/dusty rose diamond print blouse
Dark plum pants
Dark mauve bulky sweater with cowl collar
Floral/tapestry print blouse
Dark cranberry pants
Light mauve/dusty rose sweater
Dusty rose light-weight raincoat
1 pair black oxfords with stack heel
1 pair light blue terry slippers

Judy

Blue/green midriff T-shirt
Yellow/green tank top (layer)
Dark grey leggin'
Teal suede/elastic belt
Green sport socks
Slate blue sack jumper
Teal/dark turquoise "baby doll" dress
Green "hue" footless tights with ankle lace
Two-tone green "kikit" top
Two-tone green mini skirt

Faded green button front shirt with drawstring waist
Tobacco/rust button front shirt with diaper pins
Green flats
Green lace-up ankle boot (9 West)

Kiyoko

Navy blue pants
Red with blue print paisley blouse
Off-white apron
Navy-blue skirt
White silk T-shirt
Navy-blue/white kimono jacket
Taupe knit jacket with black tulips
Purple silk dress
Rust floral print blouse
Navy-blue bulky cable sweater
Grey raincoat with red trim
Cream silk scarf with pink and maroon flowers
1 pair black moccasin loafers
1 pair black pumps

Marsha

Taupe skirt
Rust/orange button front blouse with faux reptile belt
Pale pink jacket
Dark green krinkle trench coat
Lavender/white floral print dress
White fischu
Light lavender tri-collar blouse
Taupe pants with reptile belt
Off-white/pink floral mock turtleneck
1 pair tobacco suede shoes
1 taupe pleated shoulder purse

Chiyo

Mustard pullover with leopard applique
Mustard knit pants

Bright yellow knee-hi's
Green/white visor cap
Gold/magenta "ethnic" print T-shirt
Matching jacket
Denim "Beverly Hills" sequenced jacket
Bright yellow knit tunic top with Mexican-like front design
1 black "bob" style wig
1 black page boy wig
1 black curly flip with tapered neck wig
1 curly redhead with side ponytail wig
1 pair black velvet flats
1 pair thong sandals with ball heel
1 black/red/green shoulder purse

Men

Nobu

Dark green work pants (khaki's)
Green with grey cotton shirt
Grey quilted vest
Blue/white/green plaid flannel shirt
Dark green/black cardigan vest
Light grey cardigan vest
2 T-shirts
2 pair light grey heavy socks
1 pair brown check slippers
1 pair construction boots (stressed out)
1 medium blue smock

Sadao

Pumpkin color polo T-shirt
Honey-brown corduroy pants
Brown/tan tweed sport coat
Belt
Cream silk pajamas
Yellow/green pants
Yellow/rust Argyle mohair cardigan

Grey/tan flannel shirt
2 V-neck undershirts
1 pair brown suede slippers
Cream saddle shoes (not two-toned)
Navy/burgundy Argyle socks
Blue/ash brown Argyle socks
1 stick Bob Kelly hair color cream
1 toothbrush
Fishing hat

Curley

Yellow/green pants
Haichimaki (cook's hat)
2 half aprons
Cane hall "roast pig" T-shirt
Yellow/green Hawaiian shirt with palm trees
Turquoise tank top
Dark green pants
Yellow/pink Hawaiian shirt with hula girls
Hot pink tank top
Beige/blue/rust terry pullover
Brown criss-cross sandals
Canvas lace up shoe
Navy-blue socks

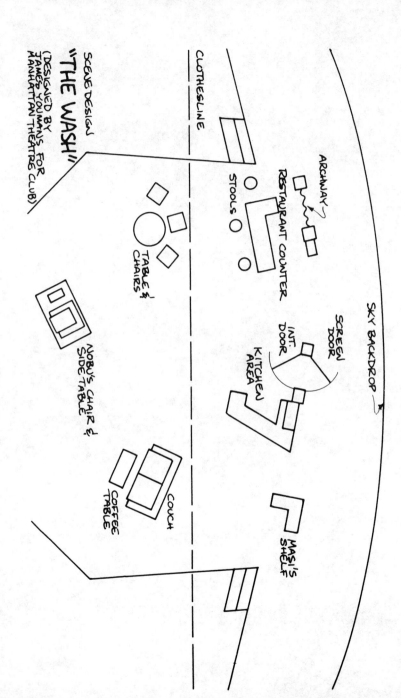

SCENE DESIGN
"THE WASH"
(DESIGNED BY
JAMES YOUMANS FOR
MANHATTAN THEATRE CLUB)

CLOTHESLINE

ARCHWAY

RESTAURANT COUNTER

STOOLS

TABLE &
CHAIRS

SKY BACKDROP

SCREEN
DOOR

INT.
DOOR

KITCHEN
AREA

NOBU'S CHAIR &
SIDE TABLE

COFFEE
TABLE

COUCH

MASI'S
SHELF

NEW
PLAYS

THE AFRICAN COMPANY PRESENTS
RICHARD III
by Carlyle Brown

EDWARD ALBEE'S
FRAGMENTS and THE MARRIAGE PLAY

IMAGINARY LIFE
by Peter Parnell

MIXED EMOTIONS
by Richard Baer

THE SWAN
by Elizabeth Egloff

*Write for information as to
availability*
DRAMATISTS PLAY SERVICE, Inc.
440 Park Avenue South   New York, N.Y. 10016

NEW
PLAYS

THE LIGHTS
by Howard Korder

THE TRIUMPH OF LOVE
by James Magruder

LATER LIFE
by A.R. Gurney

THE LOMAN FAMILY PICNIC
by Donald Margulies

A PERFECT GANESH
by Terrence McNally

SPAIN
by Romulus Linney

Write for information as to
availability
DRAMATISTS PLAY SERVICE, Inc.
440 Park Avenue South   New York, N.Y. 10016